The Sighting

Also by Luci Shaw:

Listen to the Green
Sightseers into Pilgrims (anthology)
The Risk of Birth (anthology)
The Secret Trees

The Sighting

Luci Shaw

photography by
David Singer

Harold Shaw Publishers
Wheaton, Illinois

Acknowledgements

Grateful acknowledgement is made to the editors
of the following periodicals, in which some of
these poems first appeared:
Arkenstone
The Banner
Christian Herald
Christianity & Literature
The Christian Reader
Decision
Eternity
For the Time Being
His
Interest
Kodon
The New Oxford Review
Radix
Sign
Today's Christian Woman

Design & cover photo: Kathy Lay Burrows

Library of Congress Cataloging in Publication Data

Shaw, Luci.
   The sighting.

   (The Wheaton literary series)
   I. Title. II. Series.
PS3569.H384S55   813'.54   81-9342
ISBN 0-87788-768-3   AACR2

First Printing, September 1981

to my mother

III Epiphanies

A Fore Word

John, on Patmos, opens his account of his astonishing revelation with these words from God: "Write what you see." And the description of his blazing, overwhelming vision of the Son of Man concludes with the same command from God: "Fear not . . . *write what you see*."

The words "seer" and "prophet" describe the double identity of the biblical spokesman who *sees*, looking toward heaven, receiving a vision, and then prophesies to earth and its population, *proclaiming* the oracle. The Christian poet stands alongside the seer and prophet, one foot in heaven, one on earth, trying to face in both directions at once, perpetually torn by this duality of focus as divine dreams are channelled through his eyes and ears to his voice or pen. I bear witness to the reality of the prophet's *burden*, the fearful revelation that resulted in John falling down, as dead, at his heavenly visitor's feet. Consciously or unconsciously, most of my writing has sprung from an impulse rooted in the mandate: "Fear not. Write what you see."

People perish where there is no vision. The importance of the flow of ideas and images from God is central to a biblical view of man made in God's image, in dialog with his Creator. The prophetic passages of the Bible are almost invariably accompanied by words like these: "The *vision* of Isaiah," "the *word* of the Lord, which Isaiah *saw*," "the Lord God *showed* Amos, and behold . . . ," "an *oracle* . . . the *vision* of Nahum," "the *burden* of God which Habakkuk *saw*." Ezekiel saw "*visions* of God." Daniel saw "*visions* of his head as he lay on his bed" and he was told to "write the *dream* down." We are not surprised at the reminder, in Hebrews 1, that "in many and various ways God spoke to our fathers by the prophets." But the oracle, or burden, was always mediated to the prophet by means of words or visions—what he heard, or what he saw, or both, were received from God for communication to the human audience.

But why was any intermediary, such as a prophet, needed? Why was not the Word transmitted directly, in its full blaze of light and meaning, to the whole congregation? One of the symptoms of man's degeneracy is spiritual blindness. The disease of sin has damaged his sensory receptors, and "the god of this world" has made it his high priority to distort or block man's sighting of God. Jehovah, by contrast, has become known to us as the *revealer* of "hidden" things or "mysteries" to those of his inner circle—his *cognoscenti*. In Jesus' words, "To you it has been given to know the secrets of the kingdom of heaven." Daniel sought God concerning the mystery of Nebuchadnezzar's forgotten dream, "and it was revealed to him in a vision."

But why the figurative language? Why did God not always speak openly, plainly, simply, directly, as he did through Noah or Moses or Jonah? Why mysteries? Why metaphors? Why the oblique or cryptic message? Why a special revelation through a single chosen spokesman? Why bother with a revelation at all if its meaning was not clear and accessible to the whole congregation? Why lampstands and burning swords? Why the bizarre wheels within wheels, full of eyes? Why all those unearthly beasts with their hybrid wings and horns and hooves and talons? Why the tantalizing inscrutability of vials and scrolls and bowls and seals and pale horses and scarlet women and lightnings and crystal seas and trumpets and celestial portents and white-robed multitudes? Why not simply that grand voice from heaven declaring, like a flourish of many trumpets, the truth of God and the will of God for all to hear and understand? Why *imagery?*

Any serious poet will recognize such a question as the one he is frequently asked by a world attuned to the simple declarative prose statement, by a prosaic populace for whom the computer print-out has become the one authoritative Word. For many, metaphorical writing is as mysterious as the symbolism of the Revelation. Poets and propets have always had overlapping roles. Both do double duty as receivers and transmitters of divinely conceived truth often disguised as enigma. We are told in Hosea that God was the one who "multiplied visions and gave parables" to the prophets. It was he who prescribed the imaginative mode. Ezekiel saw himself speaking for God as a "maker of allegories." Both the Old Testament and the Revelation contain some of the most striking poetry in existence, full of extraordinarily vivid symbolic language; but while much of the imagery of the Bible clarifies (giving us pictures instead of abstract doctrines, teaching effectively by analogy) many other passages contain imagery that seems difficult or impenetrable. Why? Why such obfuscation?

Jesus gives us a clue why. The Gospel of Mark records that "with many parables he spoke the word to the people . . . he did not speak to them without a parable, though privately, to his own disciples, he explained everything." In Matthew's Gospel, Jesus' followers asked him, "Why do you speak to them in parables?" Jesus' answer: "To you it has been given to know the secrets of the kingdom of heaven, but to them it has not been given . . . Here is why I speak to them in parables: because *seeing they do not see, and hearing they do not hear,* not do they understand. With them is fulfilled the prophecy of Isaiah which says: You shall indeed hear but never understand, and you shall indeed see but never perceive. For this people's heart has grown dull and their ears heavy of hearing and *their eyes they have closed* . . . but blessed are your eyes, for they see, and your ears, for they hear."

Jesus made a clear distinction between those who *want* to hear and understand, who yearn to see and believe, and those who clap their hands over their ears or shut their eyes tightly so that no flash of illumination can enter by way of their sense organs. The implication here is that soul deafness or blindness is the result of personal choice. Ears and eyes that have been created to receive revelation have been allowed to become atrophied through disuse and the result is indifference, dullness to the brilliance of the Spirit and the colorful inner landscape of creative insight.

One of the theses of Dorothy Sayers's treatise on creativity, *The Mind of the Maker,* is that we are created to see something in our minds and make what we see because we are copies ("in the image") of a Creator who saw something in *his* mind and made it. A poet (a "maker") indwelt by the Spirit must believe that true poetic insights come ultimately from the Maker, the First Poet, who helps us all, if we will, to see things as God sees them, and apply ultimate values to what we observe.

The Bible also describes false prophets who were not informed by any beatific vision. Of such, Jehovah told Jeremiah, "They prophesy lies in my name. I did not send them, nor did I command them or speak to them. They are proclaiming to you a lying vision, worthless divination, the deceit of their own minds." But he promised Jeremiah, "If you utter what is precious, and not worthless, you shall be *as my mouth*." Jeremiah's response? "Thy words were found and I did eat them, and they were the joy and rejoicing of my heart, for I am called by thy name."

As visionaries called by God's name, we have a responsibility to discern whether our insights (*in-sights!*) line up with God's special revelation—the Holy Scriptures. Where the nihilistic artist is often a prophet of the absurd and the random, seeing only distortion, fragmentation, perversity and despair, the Christian poet is permitted a sighting of a different nature. While frankly acknowledging struggle, pain, and the reality of the ugly, by writing honestly out of the shadowed places of his own life, the believing poet affirms that anguish and disorder are fragments of a larger landscape, that God is an artist, a designer, an architect who calls us back to the strong beauty of wholeness and order and felicity in Christ. The temptation, of course, is for us to dream our own dreams, to see only what we want to see, to fall in love with our own words and the sound of our own voices, to become deaf to the voice of God and blind to his signs and symbols, to emphasize our own originality, forgetting that God is the only true *original*. That is why *The Imitation of Christ* contains a proviso within the promise: "If your heart is straight with God, *then* every creature will be to you a mirror of life and a book of holy doctrine."

Luci Shaw
West Chicago, Illinois

I
Mirrors

"Art is a mirror
not because it is the same as the object,
but because it is different . . .
A mirror is a vision of things,
not a working model of them. And the
silver seen in a mirror
is not for sale."

G. K. Chesterton
in *The Uses of Diversity*

Galilee, Easter 1979

Quietly the old lake leans
against the land,
rubbing a shoulder
along the pebbles, water-worn,
sun-warm. The lips of the waves
mouth old secrets
among the reeds.
Their edges lend the shore
a small silver. Stolid,
the brown stones move a little
in the glancing light.
The wet overlap, the shaking
of the rushes' heads,
mark a continuum
of the matter.

But will we
listen and learn,
we who walk the rough border
joining the high and the
deep? Will we feel
with our feet
the narrow margin
and sense when to stand
firm as rocks, when to
dip and rise again
and wash again,
like water,
between the green slanting
stems and over
brown boulders
warm in the sun?

Signal

I'd rather be a live snake,
   sinuous, sinister, dust
   dry but silver quick,
   the signature of an old
   sin, venomous, a target
   of boys' pebbles
than this empty lace of skin,
   this fine froth of scales,
   this coiled shadow
   of the real, this death wish
   left, paralyzed, in the crack
   of a hot rock.

odd couples

things are so often
at odds with their containers:

our cat once nested her young
in a bureau drawer

the copper kettle on the shelf
is boiling with partridge berries

my eye sips babytears that leak
over a china rim

other mixed metaphors rush
to be recognized:

that baby in the corn
crib, God in a sweaty body,

eternity spilled the third day
from a hole in the hill,

for you—a painter-plumber,
me—a poet sorting socks,

all of us, teetotallers drunk
on the Holy Ghost

The problem with reflections

In ponds, in mirrors,
my face rises like a fish.
Both reverse me
(I have never seen myself real)
but it is the pond which moves
under a tentative finger,
water wrinkled like skin.
A few seconds—it heals
leaving no scar. Gravity
irons it smooth & whole
& my image with it.
Glass, though, only smudges
at a touch, unless it shatters
beyond mending. There is
no middle way. It will not
bend. Its truthfulness
is its undoing, & mine,
leaving my splintered
likeness staring up
from all the silver
slivers underfoot. No,

I must content myself with gleams
(Narcissus had problems)
catch myself glancing,
fragmented, from the bathroom
floor, laughing from some
summer lake. How can I
be sure which is more true—to be
a cool pool, fluid, prone
to evaporation, unstable,
greenly able to laugh
at a wound, to drown a friend
& forget it? Or precise
as glass, ice brittle,
faithful & unforgiving,

so solid a silver
that a crack is forever?
Gain or lose, I'll salvage
all I can—a real view
of the sun, maybe,
in my mind's mirror—
a prism leaping through
my own transparency.

The universal apple:
In the fourteenth year, February 14

His tongue tests the waxed skin; his teeth
invade the red, crushing at every bite
a thousand cells for their sweet cider.
Without ever thinking about it, the boy knows
he is eating a way back into his feral self,
intense, white-fleshed, veined, full
of sap and seed. He is as packed with cells,
as primal, as the apple whose stalk
has dropped away, forgotten as cleanly as
his own blackened unbilical cord. Still
hungry, he sizes up another apple to juggle
in the air, to rescue from its brief,
ungainly orbit, to hold with ardor, its hard,
heart shape robust as any girl's between
his palms. Richer than a printed valentine,
the earnest crimson captures all his senses,
incarnate and incarnadine. Its wholeness
circles his own core. But curiosity
conquers esthetics: pocket-knife slicing,
jagged, along its equator, he dissects
the small planet, laying its northern hemi-
sphere back on its buttock. And there,
from the center of its gravity,
all five valves filled with secret semen,
shines every schoolboy's model for a star.

Antique Shop, East Petersburg, Illinois

The sign: Four Rooms of Antiques
speaks crooked through the bungalow window.
Over the door the bell rings its treble magic,
an exchange—one storey's worth of cool
and stale and dim for a sky full of July
heat. "Too hot for *anyone* to be outside!"
(Multiple angles of old wood soak up
my small complaint.) "Yep, well now,
the farmers *need* all thet heat to bring
the corn up." His voice creaks like the floorboards
of all four rooms where the smell of must
shapes the space. Seatless or frayed, pine
chairs congregate in corners, climb to the ceiling.
And there are jars of loose brass buttons,
detached pearl and tortoiseshell buckles,
willow pattern worn past the glaze, brittle
coin silver spoons, empty mason jars bluegreen
as water that say Perfect and Kerr and Ball,
faded books full of mold and old truth, crystal
salt cellars $15 the set (without salt), thimbles,
also flat irons, pestles, spindles, clamps,
pressed glass piled like careless diamonds,
planes, whiffletrees, horseshoes rusting out
their good luck, old knives; shoot! hiding
somewhere in this room maybe there's a
doorknob once turned by Mr. Lincoln himself.

I choose a small, pale, iridescent glass bottle
marked Dr. Brand's New Discovery, two brass
drawer pulls and a clay crock and pay in the
kitchen—not a woman's room—overrun with
other people's treasures gone to dust, the once
new and cheap turned quaint and costly, all
the real values mixed and stacked, discarded or
saved, like old shelves in a cast iron bathtub.

Cramped into the corner beside the sink
stained with cigarette ends and coffee, he
is as antique as anything he sells. Joints
moving hard, skin varnished with neglect,
lips like knotted worms folded lower over
upper to hid the gaps, voicebox rotting like
an old camera bellows, the skull polished as a
china pitcher, this cracked bell of a man
stares at me without blinking, still enough
in his chair for someone to stick a round white
label on his elbow and write his price on it.

Like us

The petals on winter candles
grow from their seeds of light
up to a warmth that softens
the dark, hides the stain
on the sofa, kindles coals
in any eye
joined to their felicity.

They are time's victims
softened, like all of us,
by their own yellow heat,
uncertain in a wind,
annulled by lightning,
eating themselves toward
extinction (unless
their flickering ignites
new wicks behind
the eyelids of the mind.)

That the glory may be of God

Romans 10:20-21; 2 Cor. 4:7

Each day he seems to shine
from the more primitive pots
the battered bowls

Service may polish silver &
gold up to honor
& I could cry to glitter
like porcelain
or lead crystal

But light is a clearer
contrast through my cracks
& flame is cleaner seen
if its container
does not compete

Baudelaire

life
having been what it had
he planned revenge

his dark anger, long
asleep under the hill
like a gravid she-bear,
wakened in spring,
moved
into the light—
huge, untamed, muddying
ponds, trampling the young
green, eating
its own weight in garbage
to reproduce itself

it left him, then, alone
(spent, empty as a
winter cave) to collapse
into his own
hollowness

Theory

Some say

birds on harpsichords
plus all the time
in the world
could have sounded
the Goldberg variations

or monkeys on
typewriters
could have come out
Dante

I say

God *had*
all the time
in the world
but didn't
need it

to orchestrate us all
and write us real
in black
and white

For Grace MacFarlane—pianist

on entering a New Year

Your heart having heard heaven's
patterns of colored sound, you
have fingered them into our listening.
Spinner of song satin, your weavings
warm our naked lives, line with light
the dullest of our dreams. When you scale
ebony and ivory, all the music
comes out green.

This new year of yours—
(loomed of love, woven
with will of God)—may all
its shining length
reflect the yet-undiscovered
greens of Grace.

After divorce

for Lanny

The in-between is hard,
the mid-air, the limbo
between bank
and bank,
the long leap (legs
flailing, body un-
grounded, askew in space)
the scare
of alien air,
the interval of being
in no place,
having no where.

With love left behind,
an uncertain landing waits.
Suspended,
mind
anticipates,
feels the fall—feet first
on firm sod, or (up-ended,
unbalanced, off-guard)
slipping on a cruel
gravel. Yes.
It is the in-between
that is hard.

Fire place

"Citizens protest destruction of ancient landmark."
—newspaper headline

In one winter evening's fire
the years vanish.

The clear, concentric rings
focused at the log's core
rise, dissolved in a dream
of smoke.

The record of a century's
weather in the woods
falls in a fine, unreadable ash.

Like death, divorce and other
violence, it is a kind of
vandalism:

who can rebuild a forest,
reclaim a heart's wood?

To a poet who sees through a glass, darkly

There is mud on your shoes,
a cut on your upper lip.

Awkward with bat and ball,
foreign to politics,
surviving a small marriage
with the bare minimum
of grace & wit,
when we expect of you
a dance
we see a shuffle.
Tell me, my friend, my
fellow—Where
do your visions come from?
Does the earth ever
tremble under you?
And do the stars
still sing?

Generalization

They write of
anomalies—
the exceptional weather,
the brain-damaged child,
the unclear epiphany of a
sub-atomic particle.

How can poets generalize
except to see themselves
and say:
we are all
anomalous?

a wind chime, for seers

For Madeleine L'Engle on
the publication of A Swiftly Tilting
Planet *and* The Weather of the Heart

We'll kythe it together;
in the song of the winds
of the world as they span it
(at the touch of an air
like a feather,
the tinkle of granite)
we'll discern the heart's weather,
the balance and tilt
of the planet.

Gifts for my girl

to my youngest daughter, Kristin

At eleven, you need new shoes
often, and I would give you
other things to stand on
that are handsome and useful
and fit you well, that are not
all plastic, that are real
and knowable and leather-
hard, things that will move
with you and breathe rain
or air, and wear
well in all weather.

For beauty, I would buy
a gem for you from the earth's
heart and a ring that is gold
clear through and clothes the colors
of flowers. I would cultivate in you
a gentle spirit, and curiosity,
and wonder in your eyes. For use,
in your house I'd hang
doors that are solid wood
without hidden panels of air, set
in walls built of brick more
than one inch thick.
On your floors I'd stretch fleeces
from black sheep's backs
and for your sleep, sheets
spun from fibers that grew, once,
on the flanks of the fields.
I'd mount for you one small,
clean mirror for a grinning
glimpse at yourself, and a whole
geometry of windows to the world,
with sashes that open hard, but

once lifted, let in a breath
of pure sun, the smell of a day,
a taste of wild wind, an earful
of green music.

At eleven, and always,
you will need to be nourished.
For your mind—poems and plays, words
on the pages of a thousand books:
Deuteronomy, Dante and Donne,
Hosea and Hopkins, L'Engle and Lewis.
For your spirit, mysteries and praise,
sureties and prayer. For your teeth
and tongue, real bread the color
of grain at a feast, baked and broken
fresh each day, apricots and raisins,
cheese and olive oil and honey
that live bees have brought
from the orchard. For drink
I'd pour you a wine
that remembers sun and shadow
on the hillside where it grew,
and spring water wet enough
to slake your forever thirst.

At eleven, the air around you
is full of calls and strange
directions. Choices pull at you
and a confusion of dreams.
And I would show you a true compass
and how to use, it, and a sun steady
in its orbit and a way
through the woods by a path
that will not peter out.

At eleven you know well
the sound of love's voice
and you have, already, hands

and a heart and a mouth
that can answer. And I
would learn with you
more of how love gives and receives,
both, with both palms open. I
am standing here, far enough away
for you to stretch and breathe,
close enough to shield you from
some of the chill and to tell you
of a comfort that is
stronger, more real,
that will come closer still.

II
Windows

"What could be more mystical
or magical than ordinary daylight
coming in through an
ordinary window? . . . Why should not
that wonderful white fire,
breaking through the window, inspire
us every day like an
ever-returning miracle? . . . The mere
fact of existence and
experience is a perpetual portent.
Why should we ever ask for more?"

G. K. Chesterton
in *The Common Man*

The young girl's thoughts of birds

the young girl's thoughts of birds
flower from her head like leaves
in four directions

she is their stalk
the meanings of wings rise
in her veins like sap

four bird spirits fly
from her mind into the white air
around her

in a corona of feathers
their eyes shine like berries
like black beads rimmed with gold

their yellow beaks point
the widening compass of her inner
and outer worlds

Written after seeing a woodcut with the same
title, by Kenojuak, a Cape Dorset Eskimo, in
an exhibit of Inuit art at the McMichael
Collection in Kleinburg, Ontario.

Cosmos

"Oh now release
And let her out into the seamless world . . ."
"The Magician & the Dryad," C. S. Lewis

The crust is seamless. Though it shows
its scheme of cracks and geographic tracings, though
it trembles often from within or crumbles at its edges
as streams and oceans wear at it,
yet no man's ruthless stitching of a border,
no careless change of politics can wall
this earth from *that,* save shallowly. Fences rust.
Surveyors die. Markings fade on the maps.
Montagu falls in love with Capulet. Rains
fall on us all alike in autumn and in spring,
washing away the lines. The grass roots cross
and kiss under the hedgerows, telling us
we are kin.

Anticipation

I have come
more than a thousand miles

to race down to the shore
(lungs sampling the waves of air,
eyes unsatisfied all the way down
through scrub pine, beach plum,
indomitable grass) to see
the sea.

But the evening is flat—tide
out—nothing to catch the senses
but coarse sand
pocked with a late rain
and far, far, the knife edge
of the salt ebb.

The Atlantic
has never been tame. I discover,
with surprise, that I am not
as disappointed
at its non-response
as if it were rising fast,
hissing black, to my desire.

Bare Roofs

" . . . though I am barren, yet no man can doubt
I am clean. . . ."   C. S. Lewis

Against the sky their angles lean.
Their straight, steep pitch is rarely green.
A metaphor is plainly seen:

The roofs will not accept the rain;
they let it run away again
into the gutters, down the drain,

showing the trees their splendid sheen.
It does not do to be too clean
if you have dreams of growing green.

fear of flying: double vision

as the earth drops away
air currents fold
over the skin of
the bird I am flying / the magazines
fall open in my lap
abstractions & literary esoterica
jet stream through
mind & body at 36000 feet

in a new dimension
buffetted inside & out
I plot an erratic course
through my own cross currents / ideas
blossom in my inner troposphere
purple like the mushroom clouds
glowing around me
on the universal threshold

my husband is flying
his book / unaware of
my dangerous altitude
these solar landscapes

the possibilities are infinite
the choices few
I swallow twice / all
my antennae are out & should be
pulled back but
I am a seer & must endure
second sight

suddenly the sun is unlidded
its golden iris surrounds
the bottomless pit in my vision
I look away to the distance
of my mind / without arrogance

I am certain of a cosmos
centered at this
reclining seat

my senses are moving
the stars

rapture

driving: Bach
at work on FM
his final voice
unfaltering
cut off mid-
phrase

through the
windshield
sings the blue
well of sky

the finale is flying
flying
up there
still
soli gloria deo

hope redeems
my earthbound
progress: I
shall hear
Bach whole
and sing
with him
the new song
the infinite
fugue
he is working on

*At his death, Johann Sebastian
Bach was composing the final
contrapunta in a set of 18 entitled
"The Art of Fugue." As with
many of his musical scores it was
marked* Soli gloria deo—*"glory to
God alone."*

North St. Vrain Creek, Colorado

" . . . the creek rests the eye, a haven, a breast."
—Annie Dillard

Between fringed banks she mounds, breasting
over waterbottom, shadownippled, naked, skinned
with sky and aspen leaves and dragonflies,
bellying between the shining boulders, a fluid
flesh but firm with the force of her going.
From the bridge at noon the heat of his seeing
knuckles down at her. Senses jump the gap;
his eyes drink until the cool pools in his brain,
soaks down the thirsty length of him. As she
has found an interval's home in his eye, he
has discovered haven from the day's blaze
in her body of water.

Matrix

Some poems
open carefully
in a quiet mind,
like those oriental clamshells,
full of dry magic,
dropped into waterglass
to spread
the brilliant enamel of
their weightless petals,
frail, without seeds,

unlike those
random thoughts thrown
into the wind
that fall
to green places,
that die & shoot & blaze
& shiver in the high
morning, ready to write
their spores
into the next breeze.

Folly at East Brewster, June 1976

That morning, after the rain
   had turned the air as thin
   as innocence,
   I thought I saw three prayers
   rise singly
   over the shingled cottage roof
   like white transparent parachutes
   caught in the blue sea-wind
   and carried toward a vanishing point
   above the Monomoy horizon.

It would have seemed a fantasy
   but for the shred of silk, a
   gleam collapsed and shrunk to
   evening anonymity,
   found lying beside the path
   that leads down, solitary,
   to the far water's edge.

Report

"Recent studies show
there's always
a fair number of bees
that are lazy,
just loaf around all
the time, don't do
a damn thing."

Thus a reader's report in
The Scientific American.
Next thing, we'll
be hearing about
reasonable mules,
awkward cats,
myopic eagles,
perfect people.

The meaning of oaks I

for Doug Comstock

It is light that tugs,
that teaches each
acorn to defy the pull
down, to interrupt
horizontal space.
And falling, filtering
through the leaves
it is rain that rises,
then, like a spring
at a sapling's heart.
It is wind that trains,
toughens the wood.
It is time that spreads
the grain in rings—
dark ripples in a
slow pond.

The oaks learn slowly,
well, twisting
up, around and out,
finding the
new directions of
the old pattern branded
in each branch,
compacting, a wood
dense enough for men
to craft into a crib
for a new born, a cross
for pain, a table
for bread and wine, a door
for day light.

The meaning of oaks II

Like the unblinded man,
see the trees walking,

See
oaks and people, planted,
rooting, leafing out,
a sign in spring, a
summershade, in fall
a glory,

But observe them
most truly in winter,
naked, elemental, precise
as bones in a hand
reaching out.

" . . . let him hear."

October, 1979

All
our ears are blunt,
hot-blooded. We listen
for no call.
But this is the day
the trees obey
God & the season,
line the wood, wall
to wall, with gold
leaf, facet the view,
fleck the sun's eye
with motes that
fall   &   fall   &   fall.

Less
than maple leaves,
our ears are thicker.
How can we hear him bless
the branches with
his secret word—*Down fall*
so that the still air
dances? We confess
all we can do
is cock our heads
to catch the leaves' thin
whispered answer:
yes   &   yes   &   yes.

Counterpoint: March 21

for Kathleen Deck

Bach's birthday—and as
the vernal equinox
presents herself,
the wind's gratuitous
gifts are delivered,
white, wet,
in random bursts against
the studio windows.
Behind the blurred panes
the measured felicity
of scherzo and sarabande
is sheltered from
the intemperate insult
out of the north.

Looking out is like
wearing spectacles
in the teeth of a storm:
streaked with melting
stars, the glass distorts
a landscape that we strain
to see clear.
The unseasonal
monotony of white
blunts all the sharp
crescendos of color,
blanketing Spring's
baroque bloom
with an irrational snow.

It is Bach's birthday.
Viewing the rude weather
from the conservatory,

we glory in greener
gifts: a continuo
of order and clarity,
a music patterned for
delight, its contrapuntal
voices moving, unhurried,
through preludes, fugues
and other intricacies,
and the warm, civilized
precision of organ,
flute, harpsichord.

Remember for me

Where it was once all
birds unafraid and
wild grass and patriarchal
oaks through the window,
the developers
are sending in their
concrete armies, the ranks
of billboards.
Highways have replaced
the hidden paths.

But in the front hall
the pots of dried pods,
berries, bittersweet,
brambles, gathered
four years back
remember for me
the fires of autumn
in the fields,
the quiet rains
of spring.

Villanelle for a season's end

Autumn is here and summer will not stay.
The season cuts a bloodline on the land
And all earth's singing green is stripped away.

Our parting drains the color from the day.
The oak leaves' red is clotting in your hand.
Autumn is here and summer will not stay.

The sea fog settles. Even noon is grey.
The light recedes as though this dusk were planned.
The green of field and tree is stripped away.

We shiver on the beach and watch the way
The berries' blood is spilled along the sand.
Autumn is here and summer will not stay.

In the chill air the knotted weed heads sway.
The waves have swept our footprints from the sand.
The green of all our fields is stripped away.

See how the wind has scattered the salt hay
Across the dunes! Too well we understand:
Autumn is here, bright summer will not stay
And all earth's love and green are stripped away.

Down fall

Leaves fall and burn two ways: first
from the flaming trees, a company
of dancers in the equinoctial down-
draught to a quick, hot sidewalk fire.

Their longer falling parallels man's
from grace: isolate, earth-bound,
frayed at all their edges, dis-
integrating, down between stems
through a sieve of roots to join
earth's small, slow, smouldering, cold,
unending fires of decay.

Does Fall go back as far as Eden?

Did Eve dance, entranced,
when the first leaves on the first oaks
turned red as wine and loosed themselves?

Did the Lord God say *Good*
to beech leaves bleached back
to primary yellow?

Did Adam rake the ground clean
and burn the leaves
after his other Garden work?

November 3

for Esther-Marie Daskalakis

Crickets
are past carding in
our summer songs.
The season
is unravelling
before our eyes, rotting
as the fabric
of the field
rots. All that is
asked of us now
is that we spin
the crumpled threads,
& weave
the filaments & fibers—
sage, burnt
umber, sapphire blue—
into a curtain for
our winter view.

Prothalamion

for Jim & Sue

How like an arch your marriage! Framed
in living stone, its gothic arrow aimed
at heaven, with Christ (its Capstone and
its Arrowhead) locking your coupled
weakness into one, the leaning
of two lives into a strength.
Thus He defines your joining's length
and width, its archetypal shape. Its meaning
is another thing: a letting in of light,
an opening to a varied landscape, planned
but yet to be explored. A paradox, for you
who doubly frame His arch may now step through
its entrance into His promised land!

Wedding psalm for Mark & Robin

Fabyan Forest Preserve, May 24, 1980

Oh, may your celebration bless the Lord!
Oil in these dozen lanterns burns for you,
circling your two living wicks of love. High
in the shadows, each small tongue
of fire dances, lifts to you now its light. Hung
with its banners of spring green,
this tree-cathedral is your wedding scene,
buttressed with branches, ceilinged with sky.
Through all its airy windows, open wide,
an evening incense breathes, a heavy scent
of sweet grass freshly-cut, meant
for your nostrils. Listen. From every side
the loud frog-songs, the cricket choirs sound
antiphonally for your ears. The gilded ground,
the leafy surface of the river, each unfolds
an aisle before your feet, marrying greens and golds.

Lord, they are yours, these two. Firm in your riverbank
plant them today. In union, interweave their roots.
Anchor their sapling strength.
Season them, sun-and-shadow them, at length
ripen in them your Spirit's nine sweet fruits.
Summer them in the kindness of your heat.
Spread far and wide their seeds.
Through every leaf and prick of light, speak to them.
By robin's wings and by all woods and weeds
and in the songs of birds, whisper your words.
Rinse them with your clean rains. Make for their feet
plain paths. Firm your rock foundation under them.
Green them with all your giving and your grace.
And for the glory of your splendid Son
ignite these two, this "two-in-one",
with benediction from your shining face.

Epithalamion

for John & Betsy
Genesis 2:21-23

As God removed the archetypal rib
for metamorphosis, John, so did he hone
from you some temporary joys
(from discipline he makes delight)
so that he might
give you back Betsy, bone of your bone.

And Betsy, waking from your
wife-initiation, knowing now truly,
for the first time, who you are,
remember, how, when the Lord God spoke,
that curving, warm bone woke
into a woman!

Lord, let now your word leap down
again, lift the old curse, restore
Eden, and innocence, and say once more
Good! Will you, who made one like
yourself and from that one made two,
join them in one again?

III
Epiphanies

"Earth's crammed with heaven,
And every common bush afire with God;
But only he who sees takes off his shoes;
The rest sit around it and pluck blackberries."

Elizabeth Barrett Browning

The Sighting

for Megs & David Singer
John 9

Out of the shame of spittle,
the scratch of dirt,
he made an anointing.

Oh, it was an agony—the gravel
in the eye, the rude slime, the brittle
clay caked on the lid.

But with the hurt
light came leaping; in the shock & shine,
abstracts took flesh & flew;

winged words like view & space,
shape & shade & green & sky,
bird & horizon & sun,

turned real in a man's eye.
Thus was truth given a face
& dark dispelled & healing done.

Cathedral

During the coldest May in memory
we drive to Salisbury. My friend
is terminal, which means
her rate of ascent is faster
than mine. As we circle the Wallops
a cloud descends and covers us,
a transfiguration that whitens
the new buds on the birches and blurs
our windshield with wet snow.

We walk the glistening black path
across the Close, circle the
Chapter House, pace the damp
gravestones that pave the Cloisters.
The heat has been turned off
inside the hollow corpus
of the cathedral (it is May) and cold
fills the huge gothic ribs. Even
the gentle light from George Herbert's
stained glass face shines silver
as ice and at Evensong the first lesson
is Deuteronomical—the Cities of
Refuge and the circumstances of sudden
death—and the second is Paul stoned
at Lystra. The voices of the choristers
lift a psalm up through the carved
clerestory, piercing our soul's spaces
with a disciplined sweetness. Yes,
their throats pattern the weight of chill
with benediction while we warm
our hands between our knees.

Outside, as the sun dies through
the thin air, the spire behind us
almost touches the sky. The snow
has melted, leaving a crystal green.

My friend is terminal. Though
we see things differently (I
cannot come with her where she is going;
she cannot wait for me) we stand
and listen as the twilight blackbird
sings clear as a choirboy
from his high, naked branch.

If your eye offends you . . .

for Jack Leax & Bob Siegel

Must I then rip out my left
eye to see truly with my right?
Can there be for me no double vision?
no sweet second sight?

I know a poet & another poet
with two eyes between them, who
see more, each with his single member
than other sightseers with two.

With that unblinded inner vision, Lord
of the world, let me see you
in focus, without eyelids. Lend me
that clearer view.

The foolishness of God

for Gerald Hawthorne
1 Cor. 1:20-25

Perform impossibilities
or perish. Thrust out now
the unseasonal ripe figs
among your leaves. Expect
the mountain to be moved.
Hate parents, friends and all
materiality. Love every enemy.
Forgive more times than seventy-
seven. Camel-like, squeeze by
into the kingdom through
the needle's eye. All fear quell.
Hack off your hand, or else,
unbloodied, go to hell.

Thus the divine unreason.
Despairing now, you cry
with earthy logic—How?
And I, your God, reply:
Leap from your weedy shallows.
Dive into the moving water.
Eyeless, learn to see
truly. Find in my folly your
true sanity. Then, Spirit-driven,
run on my narrow way, sure
as a child. Probe, hold
my unhealed hand, and
bloody, enter heaven.

A celibate epiphany

An apple is meant to be
flower & food & tree
& if it goes to rot
what
of its destiny?

See,
here is a woman, planned
to be manned:
lover & mother.
Single, she
is other
knowing only a kind
of atrophy
(even an apple's designed
to be admired & eaten
& climbed)
and who but God
can exorcise
the trauma of her
empty thighs?
Between his palms' dance
he twirls her brittle stem.
His fingers
touch her virgin hem.
His light shines,
lingers,
& all glories glance
upon her inward parts.
His purpose finds
her hearts of hearts,
conceiving Jesus
at her core
by his most
Holy Ghost. Once more,

as with lonely Mary, he
makes of her
in her own time
& in his time, his sweet
bride, also a tree
thick enough to climb
with petals
for the eye's delight
& fruit to eat.

Judas, Peter

because we are all
betrayers, taking
silver and eating
body and blood and asking
(guilty) is it I and hearing
him say yes
it would be simple for us all
to rush out
and hang ourselves

but if we find grace
to cry and wait
after the voice of morning
has crowed in our ears
clearly enough
to break our hearts
he will be there
to ask us each again
do you love me

Triad: Skull Hill

I Weight lifter

Three nails focus
the force of
the gravity
holding the whole
Pattern in place.
And in that
trinity of pain
he knows (knowing)
his own body load,
adds to it
the corpus
of our failure
and thus computes
the sum, the burden of
his Father's
heavy holiness.

II Forgive them, Father

Who was he? What
were his component
parts? Body
certainly, sectioned
before our eyes.
Mind—three words
from him
carried more portent
than all
our rabbinic rhetoric.
Spirit? But that
he had already
given back.

Did we dissect him, then,
take samples of
his blood?
We did, but were
no wiser for it.

III   Shake down

His own relief
relinquished,
from the storm
at the heart
of the world, God's
grandest thunder
firms and confirms
his glory,
shakes and shifts
the ground from under
the false prince,
settles
the center cross
deeper in its place
established since
the genesis of time
and space.
God. Lightning
has already
opened the graves,
torn the hanging
barrier to the holy,
focused our sight
(*ecce homo*) on his
most lasting light.

Two stanzas: the Eucharist

Annie Dillard speaks of Christ
corked in a bottle: carrying the wine
to communion in a pack on her back
she feels him lambent, lighting
her hidden valleys through the spaces
between her ribs. Nor can we
contain him in a cup. He is always
poured out for our congregation.
& see how he spills, hot, light,
his oceans glowing like wine
flooding all the fjords among
the bones of our continents.

Annie Dillard once asked: How
in the world can we *remember* God?
(Death forgets and we all die.)
But truly, reminders are God's
business. He will see to it,
flashing his hinder parts, now,
then, past our cut in the rock.
His metaphors are many, among them
the provided feast by which
our teeth & tongues & throats
hint to our hearts of God's body,
giving us the why of incarnation,
the how of remembrance.

Jordan River

Naaman went down seven times.
Imagine it—the skin coming
clear & soft & the heart too.
But can you vision clean Jesus
under Jordan? John Baptist did,
holding the thin white body down,
seeing it muddied as any sinner's
against river bottom, grimed
by the ground of his being.

Rising then, he surfaced, a sudden
fountain. But who would have expected
that thunderclap, the explosion of
light as the sky fell, joining itself
to him, violent, gentle, a whirr of
winged pieces witnessing his work,
his worth, shaking him until the drops
flew from his shoulders, wet & common
& holy, to sprinkle the Baptizer.

Conversion

He was a born loser,
accident-prone too;
never won a lottery,
married a girl who
couldn't cook, broke
his leg the day before
the wedding
and forgot the ring.
He was the kind
who ended up behind a post
in almost any
auditorium. Planes
he was booked to fly on
were delayed
by engine trouble
with sickening regularity.
His holidays at the beach
were almost always
ruined by rain. All
his apples turned out
wormy. His letters
came back, marked
"Moved, left no
address." And it was
his car that was cited
for speeding
from among a flock of others
going 60 in a
55 mile zone.

So it was a real shocker
when he found himself
elected, chosen by Grace
for Salvation, felt
the exhilaration of
an undeserved and wholly

unexpected Joy
and tasted, for the
first time, the Glory
of being on
the winning side.

Burden

Ezekiel 3:3; 4:4-8; 5:1, 2

How, in the body of the prophet,
is enacted the Word
of the Lord! Ezekiel lies bound,
face forward to the besieged city,
a day for a year—
on his left side for the
stubbornness of Israel, three
hundred ninety days, forty
days for rebel Judah
on his right—
bearing their burden, the Word
a weight like a stone
in his stomach.

So does God's metaphor approach
his purpose: Word
embodied, Breath from heaven
given bone and blood,
lying prone or walking heavily
on dusty feet; dark vision
turned to speech in a man's mouth.

Head and beard razed, hair
weighed and divided in thirds
for destruction: this
is Jerusalem,
burned, scattered, pillaged.
So is the Word become flesh.

Benediction: the grace of salt

The spring stars thicken like brine
toward their zenith; sand
in July sifts through our shoes
along the beach road, a saline pricking
between the toes at seas' edge;
across the lower field in fall each twig
& blade shines crystalline with frost;
and our lips lift to the bite, the cold salute
of a winter seasoning
as the world is salted with snow.

All the earth is white with the salt of the Lord!
Observing this, the Hebrews
sprinkled their sacrifices & their newly born
for blessing. Ancient covenants
in Israel were ratified with the holy grains,
friend bonded to friend.

Caution! the heavens are shaking again:
we taste the fine tang in the air
with tongues anxious for the sting of white
to scour our souls
& heal our bitter springs
& season us with fire.

Benedicite. O Lord
by thy grace preserve us!

John, the Sent One

John 1:37-40; Luke 9:58; Revelation 1:17

The fox
borrows a burrow;
earth, sea & air
are the gulls'
three homes.

My limewashed walls
are blank canvasses,
my visions
thick enough
to be painted
into life, there,
secure inside
the solid shelter
by the shore

until I remember:
the son of man
has nowhere.

Star song

We have been having
epiphanies, like suns,
all this year long.
And now, at its close
when the planets
are shining through frost,
light runs like music
in the bones,
and the heart keeps rising
at the sound of any song.
An old magic flows
in the silver calling
of a bell,
rounding
high and clear,
flying, falling,
sounding
the death knell
of our old year,
telling the new appearing
of Christ, our Morning Star.

Now burst,
all our bell throats!
Toll,
every clapper tongue!
Stun the still night.
Jesus himself gleams through
our high heart notes
(it is no fable).
It is he whose light
glistens in each song sung
and in the true
coming together again
to the stable,
of all of us: shepherds,

sages, his women and men,
common and faithful,
wealthy and wise,
with carillon hearts
and suddenly, stars in our eyes.

Bethany Chapel

Bracketed between the first
tentative prayers, a silence fills
this place, a shadowed listening
as our separateness seeks out
the Spirit's focus for this hour
and gathers strength enough
to peer and soar
into small, shining arcs of praise
held at their lower ends
by the old hymns. Christ
in this crowd of rest and rising
humbles himself again to our
humanity; and like the sheep
(trembling in the shearer's hands)
surrenders to us once more
in quietness.

As at his dark birth and death
we had his body in our fingers,
now, again, we split the whiteness
of his loaf by turns, and tasting
his imaged life against
the cup's cool rim
we take him in.
Nourished by that final flesh,
that ultimate blood behind
the chosen signs, our God-thoughts,
seeds of worship, multiply to words.
Light flows down to us, and back,
joins us in one body of fire—
one polyphon of light now
sounding out himself—
one flame of singing
burning into being.

other books in the **Wheaton Literary Series:**

The Achievement of C. S. Lewis, by Thomas Howard. "Written with Lewis's own passionate power with words."—*Peter Kreeft.* Paper, 196 pages

Adam, by David Bolt. An imaginative retelling of the Genesis 1-3 narrative. "I think it splendid."—*C. S. Lewis.* Cloth, 143 pages

Creation in Christ: Unspoken Sermons, by George MacDonald, edited by Rolland Hein. Devotional essays revealing a deeply moving understanding of holiness and man's relationship to God. Paper, 342 pages

Geometries of Light, poems by Eugene Warren. "He shows how abundantly love has poured Itself into our 'seed-filled light' and 'night-locked flesh.' "—*Robert Siegel.* Paper, 108 pages

A Guide Through Narnia, by Martha C. Sammons. A detailed study of Lewis and his Chronicles of Narnia, with map, chronology and index of names and places. Paper, 165 pages

Images of Salvation in the Fiction of C. S. Lewis, by Clyde S. Kilby. Explores the Christian meaning in Lewis's juvenile and adult fiction. Cloth, 140 pages

Life Essential: The Hope of the Gospel, by George MacDonald, edited by Rolland Hein. "A book for those who hunger after righteousness."—*Corbin S. Carnell.* Paper, 102 pages

Listen to the Green, poems by Luci Shaw. Poems that see through nature and human nature to God. Illustrated with photographs. Paper, 93 pages

The Miracles of Our Lord, by George MacDonald, edited by Rolland Hein. "A better set of meditations on the miracles of Christ would be hard to find."—*Walter Elwell.* Paper, 170 pages

The Secret Trees, poems by Luci Shaw. "These are the real thing, true poems . . . they work by magic."—*Calvin Linton.* Cloth, 79 pages

Tolkien and the Silmarillion, by Clyde S. Kilby. A fascinating view of Tolkien as a scholar, writer, creator and Christian, based on Kilby's close association during the collation of the Silmarillion. Cloth, 89 pages

Walking on Water: Reflections on Faith and Art, by Madeleine L'Engle. Shows us the impact of the Word on words and ourselves as co-creators with God. Cloth, 198 pages

The Weather of the Heart, poems by Madeleine L'Engle. "Read her poetry and be chastened and filled with joy."—*Thomas Howard.* Cloth, 96 pages

The World of George MacDonald: Selections from his Works of Fiction, edited by Rolland Hein. "A treasure of a book—one to be read and reread." —*Frank E. Gaebelein.* Paper, 199 pages

Available from your local bookstore, or from
HAROLD SHAW PUBLISHERS
Box 567, Wheaton, IL 60187